WHAT REALLY HAPPENS
Behind the CHURCH DOORS

Pastor Willie D. Brown

TABLE OF CONTENTS

FOREWORD

Bishop Tommie L. Triplett, Jr.
Senior Pastor/Teacher

"One Church in Two Locations"

Contact Information

2100 Ames Blvd.
Marrero, LA. 70072
504-347-6424

2401 Annette St.
New Orleans, LA. 70119
504-949-2559
Fax: 504-341-3414

Ministry Links

Email Address
unitedfellowshipfgbc@yahoo.com

Website
www.unitedfellowship.org

Facebook Address
www.facebook.com/unitedfellowship

Twitter Address
@uffgbc

Our Mission

*Empowering the Church
Enabling the Community
Embracing the Kingdom*

I have watched this great man of God from his adolescent years and he has continued to strive toward excellence in doing the work of the Kingdom of God. Even then you could see God's hand on him ordering his steps. In his book, *"What Really Happens Behind the Church Doors,"* Pastor Willie (Duke) Brown offers a masterful way of delivering witty words that are laced with truth. Have you ever wondered what goes on behind the doors of the church?

In this book, Pastor Brown exposes the attacks of the enemy that he experienced in the freshman years of his ministry. He effortlessly uses his journey to lead his readers into understanding that no matter what comes your way you must never allow anything to hinder or cancel your destiny. Through transparency Pastor Brown unravels moments of tragedy that evolved into moments of triumph. The life lessons in this book are invaluable to the new pastor in reaching a palatial level of maturity in ministry.

In *"What Really Happens Behind the Church Doors,"* seasoned preachers will attest to the challenges that pastors face while doing ministry. Young preachers will gather the necessary insight to navigate through the path of learning to lead the flock of God, while anticipating the coming attractions of ministry. Pastor Brown provides wisdom for the laity that will help them understand the path and pitfalls of pastoring while incorporating the need for their support.

Pastor Brown is on the fast track in ministry with this wonderful orchestrated piece of literature and he provides pastoral precision with professional candor.

This book is a must have for anyone who wants to reach their destiny in pastoral leadership and for those who want to traverse through the (sometimes) torrential waters of ministry. Therefore, I am convinced that everyone should have a copy of *"What Really Happens Behind the Church Doors."*

Bishop Tommie L. Triplett, Jr.
Senior Pastor/Teacher
United Fellowship Full Gospel Baptist Church
New Orleans, Louisiana

"What Really Happens Behind the Church Doors"

DEDICATIONS

This book is dedicated to the Memory of my Maternal Molders who were monumental in my mentoring and Ministry. To my late Mother, Camella "Mel Baby" Brown, who never failed to let the world know, "that's MY son." So many of my traits and radiant personality to draw people in masses comes from her spirit that still resonates today in Vacation Bible School record attendance at our childhood home Church, Macedonia Baptist Church, in East St. Louis, IL. My personality is a testament to her legacy and pure passion for people persistency.

To my beloved Grandmother, the late Claudia "Boopie" Watson-Jackson who raised me as a son/grandson, in that order, from toddler to adult. Honestly, I never called her anything but "Mama" and eventually the nickname I gave her as an adult, "My Boopie." I often tell people that she raised me my first 20 years and I took care of her the second 20 years, until God ultimately promoted her to be with Him. Boopie was never just my Grandmother, she was my best friend, sustainer and solid supporter. My Boopie knew, her Baby Boy would never see her want for anything and would gladly sacrifice everything to keep his word as his integrity was a part of his reality. Praise GOD for the solid, strong women who kept me on the straight and narrow to stay on the course of my GOD ordained destiny, which they saw from the day I arrived. In addition to the maternal memory dedication, this book is also dedicated to those who have had monumental and incomparable impacts on my life.

To the Love of my life, inclusive of my heart, mind and soul, my God Daughter and baby girl forever, Lady Tyra J. Suggs, "aka" "Heaven". Her name for me, from God, was "Heaven" as she was my gift directly from His door. Even more, God revealed an arsenal of awesome anointing and attachments in her for which He had assigned me accountability from birth to fruition.

To my best friend, right hand and arm throughout my jolted and joyful journey Lady Catherine Suggs.

To my Baby Sister, Claudia "Penny" Brown, who has been by my side since birth and been her Brother's biggest fan, even more, solid supporter throughout the ride. I simply call her "my Mama's last child" and tell her often that God saved the Best Child to be the last child.

There were so many who truly aided and assisted: Kenneth Dean Leek, the late Mrs. A.D. Sampson and Mrs. Alma Jean Johnson. To my Ministerial mentor Pastor Earl A. Griffin, Bishop Tommie L. Triplett, Jr., God Parents Deacon John and Mama Bonnie Snowden, adopted Dad/ Father CMSgt (Ret) Harold "Ray" Collins, CCMSgt (Ret) Anthony "Chief" Brinkley, Dr. Gordon D. & Brenda Bush and my newly adopted parents Steven & Min. Brenda Jackson; just to name a few of the most influential persons.

All Glory to GOD for pouring His providential path to connect the dots needed for my God ordained destiny.

INTRODUCTION

As you begin to travel this true life Joseph journey, buckle up for a full and inclusive glass of many of the situations and sagas which lie beneath surface view. This book shares my life from an inner city kid in the hood to a present young Pastor who's experienced a taste of the good, bad and ugly which lies behind the church walls. My story is shared in dynamic depth and detail with an all-inclusive "tell all" of the joys and jolts of the journey which precedes destiny.

Understanding the Full Story of what "really" happens behind the church doors means addressing the reality and spirituality contained in the total package. In your reading of "What Really Happens Behind the Church Doors," you will discover in-depth, those things not seen on the surface and only revealed behind the scenes.

This book reveals the whole truth and nothing but the truth. As a Pastor or Leader, just as Jesus himself experienced, every destiny is preceded by a dark hour moment. Behind the doors, expect to experience Deliverance but also expect to encounter Delilahs and persistently pray that you flee flesh so that you'll be a Joseph example, leaving the shirt, and not a David disappointment, looking and lusting into a devastating dilemma which results in death and doom. Also prepare for departures from persons who would rather leave than be led and pass on positive participation if not afforded key positions. Ministry is indeed tough but when laced with integrity, you will be rewarded with Favor for your Faithfulness. You'll never find another book that goes INSIDE out and flows from start to finish. Prepare for a Flight you'll never forget as this Pastor/ Playwright paints the picture of providence pouring into your Destiny residence unlike anything our Planet has ever witnessed to date.

Chapter One

HOW IT ALL BEGAN

One of the most common statements I remember growing up in the traditional Missionary Baptist Church after hearing the Sermon was, "the doors of the Church are now open." I often wondered from a Biblical perspective, "Spiritually, do the doors ever close?" as our kingdom responsibility is never complete until Christ returns to take us to our "real" home."

I knew raising that discussion topic to adults as a kid was probably not the best idea in a season where a child stayed in a child's place. Ironically, raising this issue as an adult now presents a perfect parallel to present the platform for this book. When we physically join the Church, thereby entering the doors of the Church which have been "publicly" opened in our Worship experience, how much does this even remotely resemble the "private" portions which is happening behind the doors and ultimately have the most impact?

On the surface, we enter what appears to be wide open loving arms, unconditional pure love, uninhibited, radical Praise and a feeling of family forever, for always, for love. However, you will soon discover that entrance intro to be a "honeymoon" moment and rarely ever a lifetime experience. In this book, I will share a real life journey of the joys and jolts, fluctuations and deviations, mountains and valleys, facts and fictions but most of all, an all-inclusive picture of what often comes "after" you enter those doors. Buckle up for a flight inclusive of the total package as it relates to participation and parking on the inner premises.

Allow me to go back to the roots that led to my path from pupil to parishioner; a big afro kid Preacher to a seasoned Senior Pastor who has been through the fire, and the flood while experiencing the Favor from being faithful "throughout" the ride.

It was clear to me at a very young age that there was a calling on my life. Growing up in an inner city neighborhood, widely referred to as "Golden Gardens", the opportunity for my life to be the exact opposite of promise and positive was abundant.

My abundance lied in parking in positive potential; versus landing upon a sad, statistical destiny of drowning in doom and degradation. I could follow the polluted path of some peers in keeping pace with the sad and sickening statistics of drugs, alcohol, gangs, and even death; or I could proceed providentially and seek my Divine Purpose in GOD; while watching Him direct my path.

As a kid, I loved to clown and had no problem being referred to as class comedian, class clown or crazy "Duke". This is the nickname given to me by my Grandmother. Those references might have authentically applied at the time, but I was never a fool. I knew it would behoove me, mainly my backside, to complete my academic requirements with excellence before creating the stage when my teachers stepped out the room. I disrupted the class every chance I got, during the teacher's absence.

Ironically, as a child, I thought my peers had the problem in not completing work assignments prior to joining my entertainment audience. After all, if they were foolish enough to watch me perform live on the classroom stage during a major exam or timed California Achievement Test, they were CRAZY!

I now stand as a living witness for correction and direction as my beloved mother, and adored grandmother helped aid and assist me in understanding the distraction dynamic, as they applied the Board of Education to my seat of understanding.

As I approached the double digits in childhood, I grew more and more intensely interested in the Word of God; reading and understanding it. I became more interested daily in passionately possessing a zeal, to not only learn it, but also teach it and preach it to anyone and everyone. This was not an option! Before I would play, you had to come to my side patio Church and get your WORD in my makeshift congregation.

It was a sight to behold and many of the parents were amazed at how serious we were. It was not "playing" Church. It was having Church with a WORD, Music and kids in Worship. Our Kid Church was probably one of the first KID Interdenominational Church's ever; as our first members consisted of kids from families of Catholic, Methodist, Baptist and Church of God in Christ (COGIC) backgrounds.

As I mentioned earlier, getting my participation in playing sports and games, the prerequisite of coming to our Kid Church was a non-negotiable option. Being a gifted athlete with great leaping ability for basketball, physical aggression for making contact in football and any other sport, my participation was preceded by what could be called a "peer convocation" at our Kid Church. My life began to shift from Kid Church to a much more serious spiritual assignment as I sensed the supernatural calling coming from my Creator. From the age of seven, I knew it was something different about me and I ignored and fought what I knew because of the fear of my calling being rejected because of my age.

As I entered my teen years, I could see I had spiritually received a divine dispatch direct from my daddy's desk. It became unbearable, yet crystal clear to me that this child of the cloth calling was not something I would be able to blow off and simply dispose into a dumpster of denial, but it had to be addressed and accepted. After years of my giving GOD a Jonah response, I accepted my calling into the Gospel Ministry to preach the Gospel. From the day I surrendered and submitted, there was a relief which equated to the feeling and exhausting emotion of a 500 pound weight being lifted off my chest.

The "formal" preaching chapter of my ministry began with me traveling around the country preaching and singing, during 5-7 day revivals as Special Guest Evangelist and facilitating Youth Workshops. I was always full of energy with an Eveready Bunny spirit to stay on my Gospel grind. Being licensed in a Church which had over 70 preachers did not help. Many of my fellow preachers were content with preaching once every 3 years or getting the golden opportunity to do the altar call, read the scripture or extend the

Invitation during morning worship or during the evening radio broadcast.

However, I was eager to be active and consistently engaged in exercising the multiplicity of gifts which God had birthed down in my belly. What an eye opener for me at that time, as the only opening was Youth Pastor of a local AME Church.

This was truly an experience, as a high energy Baptist boy, with a serious COGIC flava, began his first formal assignment in a conservative, "now you know it don't take all that", AME Church. One of my personal Pastoral mentors really helped me understand the blessing of what appeared to be an unbearable burden at the time. He said to me, "if you can preach in a cemetery, you'll have no problem anywhere there is any sign of life." This was much needed and most timely as my "spiritual Dad" who would afford me the opportunity to preach often, saw the sad shifting in my demeanor to dismal and disappointed; as my high spirited energy, enthusiasm, vigor and vitality was not happily received. In most cases, I was outright rejected. Yes, I was rejected right inside the doors of the church!

This eventually changed as members began to embrace me for who I was. As such, the youth increase fruits were rapidly produced as our Youth Department grew to be one of the biggest and best in the region. It was also during this first formal Ministry Introductory Tenure that I took one of the most piercing painful personal punches of my ministry. As I said earlier, my Pastor/Spiritual Dad, truly believed in me, supported me and trusted my gift and integrity to represent him anytime and anyplace.

I will never forget this monumental Ministry moment which took place on a Spring Sunday evening when he afforded me the opportunity to go to one of the Premier AME Churches in the region. This church also had one of the most popular, yet outspoken Pastors. It was a huge and historic day as they celebrated one of the greatest days in the life and legacy of their ministry, their Church Anniversary.

The people were in the place as it was jam packed with wall to wall members from throughout the AME district and other denominations from the region. The only nervous overload experience which ever even came remotely close to this day was the day I preached my first sermon or as ole school Church called it, "trial sermon". This memorable moment took place at a jam packed Macedonia Baptist Church with our Pastor and Preaching legend, Rev. Dr. Norman E. Owens, Sr., sitting and listening while conducting a candid critique of my communication, accurate information and correct impartation.

Back to that frightening moment at this wall to wall people packed Church Anniversary celebration with members twice and triple my age overflowing in the aisles. Here I sat, a teen Preacher, biting my fingernails and fighting off nervous chills, in the presence of Senior Pastors from Churches throughout the city and region, standing in as the substitute, or as they formally referred to us during that day, "alternate".

In reality, I was the "sub", but in my spirit, it felt more like the "sacrifice". Catching me totally off guard, this very popular Pastor floored me during what was supposed to be my introduction.

He did not bite his tongue as he expressed his unedited true feelings in cold and candid communication without restraint or restriction. His wounding words were, "I thought Pastor J was my friend. I can't believe he sent me a boy to do a man's job." In my initial emotion, I wanted to get up, grab my Bible and exit the pulpit stage. I was hurt, speechless and stunned.

In my Spirit, I knew I had to submit to my assigned task. I had to remember the right response and adhere to the endless echo of one of my very first Ministerial mentors and God Father, Pastor Earl A. Griffin. He would always shout throughout my sermon, "look to the hills son", and Preach the Gospel; as I had been tasked to do.

Just as I shall never forget the "remarks", I shall never forget the "release" as the Holy Spirit hit the House like a round two on the day of Pentecost as recorded in the Book of Acts. After the message, and the experience of what appeared to be a spiritual thunderstorm with ongoing lightning of explosive, potent, powerful and passionate Praise, the Pastor returned with only 2 things; offering me a public apology and secondly, asking me if I would return and conduct his Fall Revival as the featured Special Guest Evangelist for the week.

I accepted the apology and humbly accepted the invitation. It turned out to be one of the best revivals to ever take place in this town. It was this triumphant turning point which birthed preaching, speaking and singing invitation extensions to me locally, nationally and abroad.

As I traveled around the country, these preaching opportunity moments were priceless. People were intrigued with a multi-gifted, endless energized young Kid Preacher and I was blown away that GOD would call and use such an unworthy vessel such as me.

I was not only grateful and appreciative, but I was hugely humbled, unselfish and wanted other youth to experience the exposure, love and opportunity of sharing their gifts and talents abroad, which I was now receiving in abundance.

Chapter Two

THE SHIFT FROM CHILDHOOD
TO ADULTHOOD

Coming from a small inner city community, many of my peers had never even traveled across the bridge to the St. Louis Zoo.

At this time I was coming out of my teen years and now in my early 20s. My desire to share the opportunity of exposure and experience with my peers grew even more. I was led to move from talking about it, to being about it in creating the vehicle for this vision of experience, exposure and gift sharing. This spiritual impregnation had come full term as I completed a Youth Revival at a Church called Calvary in a place called Centreville, Illinois. Here another Spiritual Mentor,

Pastor Albert Collins, saw something in me and pushed me toward my potential and God's deposited gifts in me.

After this revival, God gave me a vision to expand what was called the Youth Quake Revival into a Youth Quake Mass choir. This choir was unlike any other, as youth and young adults from throughout the St. Louis Metropolitan area came to participate in singing, playing instruments, directing, and providing full blown outreach Ministry.

As this historic revival week winded down, God revealed to me that this was the beginning of something global and from this choir was birthed a very timely and much needed YOUTH Movement, which would be called the Save Our City Crusade (S.O.C.C.).

In the summer of 1988, a group of inner city youth, from the heart of the hood on both sides of the river, East St. Louis, Illinois and St. Louis, Missouri, would emerge as one of the greatest youth and young adult choirs to ever be assembled to date. There was none like SOCC and to this day, nearly every St. Louis Metro vocalist, musician, gospel recording artist, actor or mainstream talent, has come through the SOCC exchange or experienced the SOCC train.

After traveling across the country as one of the greatest Youth Gospel choirs ever, I noticed during one late evening, as SOCC was returning from a tour on our bus trip home, all of the various talents, personalities and characters in those 47 seats. I thought to myself, "what diversity and the awesome cutting edge Ministry which could come from developing a creative unity from that diversity."

I didn't quite understand it at first, but GOD was revealing next level vision and expansion for Save Our City Crusade. He revealed to me in that moment that SOCC was no longer just a choir, but that a new level and dimension of Ministry was on the horizon. The spirit led me to zoom in on the antics, actions and pay close attention to the variety of personalities. I saw those who were comedic, those who were super serious, those who were introverts, extroverts and divas in the making, just to name a few. The revelation was registering loud and clear. The next step vision would be inclusive of a Christian theatrical touring company.

It was on that day that I was led to launch the vision and structural construction plan for the Save Our City Crusade theatrical touring company.

These classic moments were humongous in humor and downright hilarious. Even though these unforgettable bus ride memories took place nearly 25 years ago, on my most dismal and dim day, I can reflect back and shift from doom to drowning in laughter.

One of those days took place as we were boarding our Charter Coach for a super long road trip to the East Coast. Talking about unforgettable, two of the largest bodies on the bus were trying to sit next to one another in these small bus seats. After both tried to play it off like this might be a viable possibility, came the crash conclusion of reality.

The big fellow finally gave up the ghost and confessed to the big lady and the entire bus, "This is NOT going to work. Ain't no way on God's green earth the two of us are going to fit in these two seats." We nearly flat lined from laughter.

Another unforgettable SOCC folly, truly in a class all by itself for most humorous moment honors, was when the largest passenger, decided to wear spandex for comfort on this long, forever and a day, bus trip. She decided she wanted an item from the overhead. She arose out of her seat and began to reach up into the overhead storage compartment to grab her item. Unfortunately, for one of our recording artist who sat directly across from her as she was slowly wakening, she knew what was happening right before her very eyes, had to be a dream that was rapidly turning into a nightmare. As she glanced over the big sister was reaching up, and tragedy was rapidly headed her way as the big sister's spandex were sliding down! From her view, it appeared that the red sea split was coming into full exposure. She couldn't take the chance, as time was of the essence. She rose up suddenly, screamed the big girls name and said, "Stop the madness, I don't need to see all that."

There was never a dull day with SOCC. Whether it was getting 3 hours away from home to a venue, only for the musician to remember he left his keyboard in the trunk of his car, on the parking lot which we departed from. Not to mention having the entire group pack as if we had a two week vacation as opposed to the actual 3 day trip to Jacksonville, Florida. We didn't have enough room for the passengers to even get down the aisle of the bus; which delayed our departure two hours as we decided the essential items versus the extreme excess.

Another moment had us sitting in the center ditch of a major interstate after our bus caught fire and forced us to vacate. After many hours of waiting for help, we got hungry and proceeded to order Pizza Hut on a cell phone. This led to the entire restaurant management team coming out to see if we were really serious, or was this a pathetic prank?

On a more serious note, having one of our members who was a severe asthmatic suffer a life threatening asthma attack while traveling cross country. After rushing to her aid only to discover the inhaler was in her luggage, under the bus, amongst 70 other pieces of luggage!

One other matchless, memorable moment occurred as we were set to do the biggest tour of our lives. Our master musician decided at the last moment, due to relationship saga with his girlfriend, he was not going!

From that day forward, not only would SOCC minister in music, we would now travel to cities throughout the country adding full theatrical presentations to our repertoire in the presentation of Gospel stage play productions at churches.

After a few years of performing in churches and many of our members growing older, the Lord showed me it was time to shift into the next season with the adults who remained engaged throughout the original theatrical chapter. The next vision platform launched the professional chapter which would expand into larger audiences with performances in theatres, major auditoriums and venues across the country. Providence and provision prevailed as the Lord opened major doors in Chicago, Atlanta, Jacksonville, Florida, Huntsville Alabama, Columbus Mississippi, Tulsa, Oklahoma and even the nation's Capital of Washington, D.C., just to name a few.

This new next level vision was activated and the WDB Professional Theatrical Touring Company was launched. This vision extension and addition expanded to 90 plus cities abroad and served as a Mobile Ministry and Pulpit altar on wheels. It was awesome and amazing as the anointing flowed from the stage into the seats.

People not only got to attend one of the greatest stage plays on tour, but were also afforded altar calls, "backstage" Church and Christian counseling when receptive and/or requested. This was the final Chapter of my Mobile Ministry and the next seasonal shifting was being birthed.

It happened on the 3rd Sunday of January of 2003, as the doors to my 1st church as a Senior Pastor were opened and after 28 years of preaching, I became a Senior Pastor.

Chapter Three

THE PASTORAL BEGINNING

Beginning a Ministry from the ground level is another level of stress, strain and struggle, especially when the announcement and opportunity comes totally unexpected. My journey began with a major Sunday shocker as the Senior Pastor at the church which I was temporarily serving as Co-Pastor, (so I thought), stunned the Sunday Morning crowd with his surprise announcement. He simply called his wife to the front of the church, who had no clue either and dropped the bomb. No one expected this and personally, I thought he was going to present her with some flowers or a special gift. His words rung like a loud boisterous Catholic Church bell in a small town when he said, "Pastor Brown never knew why he came. I always knew why he came. "I was sent to start this Ministry, but Pastor Brown was sent to continue it. I'm stepping down, and from this day forward, he's your Pastor."

The congregation went silent and everyone sat stunned and speechless. There were many responses I will never forget, especially the very first one, as one of his relatives rose up, walked out of the choir loft and voiced her displeasure with his decision. One other person shouting, "I will never call him Pastor!" Another response was from one who currently serves as the Mother of our church and even has an entire wing named in her honor. Mother took the floor and consoled me with the most comforting words ever, "Pastor Brown, this ain't about you, it's the way it was handled."

Mother would eventually remind the members who were not happy about the former Pastor's decision, to say the least, to remember I was not the one who left; I was the one who stayed.

It was a very tough turning point and decision in my life, as I was scheduled to leave the following week but never had the opportunity to share that departure information with the Pastor prior to his surprisingly sudden and unexpected resignation. Understand, I never went to this church to stay; I went to aid and assist on special assignment.

Ironically, it was in God's plan all the time. I must share the backdrop or "behind the scenes history", prior to my concurrence to serve as a temporary fill-in.

One critical point I must make is that BEFORE the Pastor presented the offer for me to come and serve 8-10 months while he tended to and addressed some major medical concerns; God had already shown me the "area". I had previously spoken to my Senior Pastor at my home church, the Rev. Dr. Obie Rush, where I served as Youth Pastor about possibly seeding a church in that area. His initial response was candid and concurring as he said he would definitely support me, but knew the arsenal of anointed gifts which had been bestowed upon me. In a very caring voice, he said, "I really think you're too gifted to have to start like that and if you're patient, it will definitely come." Then came this formal offer months later. Once this offer arrived to aid and assist in the same area we had previously discussed, Pastor Rush felt it would be great administrative experience and an excellent opportunity for me. The only odd twist in all this was that we both agreed, "if I accepted this assignment for administrative growth and Pastoral experience, I would not seed a church in this area as most of the persons who would join during my temporary tenure, would also seek to follow me as their Undershepherd, once I left since I was in the same vicinity."

The Lord truly blessed during the temporary tenure, as the Youth Department grew to be one of the largest and most visible in the Midwest.

There was an ongoing launching of initiatives which drew Youth Ministries locally and nationally with programs such as Youth Quake, Crunk 4 Christ, Pastor WDB Etiquette Excellence Conference (EEC), PWDB-TTT Teen Talk Television, Boys 2 Men Male Mentoring Conference, Gospel Apollo, and Teens in the WORD rap sessions, just to name a few. As much as the Lord had blessed, I was still in the mindset, once my tenure was complete, I was up and back to my home church until the Lord called me into a Pastorate.

The Providential twist in all this was the most important component. As I initially shared in the beginning of this chapter, I had preached at a vacant church the week prior to the Pastor's sudden resignation announcement. The vacant church had pretty much indicated that I was their choice and I had privately claimed in my heart that they were mine. What a total package blessing I thought it would have been, as they had a Music Ministry second to none and music was one of my true loves. The church also had a beautiful and spectacular spacious facility, huge edifice for growth and in-house Ministry expansion, paved parking lot on a huge corner, minimal debt and placed me in another state with opportunities to join a family of new Pastoral peers and fresh Ministry opportunities. Here was the twist, prior to the Pastor giving his abrupt resignation, I had already decided I was going to give my farewell appreciations and accept the other Pastoral opportunity for what appeared to be a Pastoral Paradise set before me. Here's a golden opportunity for me to work in the ministry full-time. I could pour my heart and soul into building the kingdom! For me it was a dream come true.

As the now departing Pastor spoke, his words leaving the congregation stunned, I was having a conversation in my spirit with GOD. I could hear God speaking into my spirit that this was not by incident, or accident but with divine intent. He pointed out to me that this was by His divine design.

I had clearly decided that I was opting for the convenience and comfort of the situation which included stability. Surely God wasn't telling me this assignment that I thought was temporary is what He had for me permanently?

I'm saying to myself, "I'm not even staying and what is this man talking about?" At the same time, God is reprimanding me in my spirit, "Did I not show you O'Fallon? Did I ask you to ask your Pastor to assist with a seed? Did I ask you to look for a building or even people? I simply showed you the area. Now you can go to what's comfortable or you can go to where I'm planting you."

It was a very tough moment, but I had to stand down and submit to the path which HE had providentially planted and divinely directed. My only comment to the congregation of which many seemed to be opposed to me stepping in as the sole Senior Pastor was, "I'm going to step away for a Sunday and let you think about it, but I will not attempt to serve anywhere I'm not wanted." In my heart, I could see that I really didn't have a choice if I was going to align with God's will." I returned the week after, assumed my assignment and the rest is history.

Chapter Four

MINISTRY GENESIS

The first year was one of revelation, as I discovered the steep hills we needed to climb just to get to minimal operational standards. First thing was purchasing the property for which the church had been leasing and recently denied financing for purchase. It was a tough season, as we were treading transition. Transition is tough and even tougher when the new leader in the forefront and lead chariot is perceived by many as an outsider. It takes true spiritual maturity for there to be smooth transition. If this maturity is not clicking in cohesion, conflict will culminate. People who are not ready to rise will present more problems than progress.

As a new Pastor or leader, you can never be afraid to lose sheep that have no desire to follow. Be very weary of those who always seek ownership, but have no followership and respect for your leadership to LEAD. They have exhibited ulterior motives and self-serving DNA by showing signs and samples of their "I" personal pronoun identity in a "we" and "us" team environment.

Stay in the Word and always revert back. Remember, Jesus left the 99 to go back and find the "lost" sheep, not a sheep who had simply decided to leave. In ministry you have to understand and immediately identify the huge difference. The difference between a sheep that lost his way as opposed to a sheep who voluntarily left. As a Shepherd, we're called to protect and cover our sheep. If the Shepherd is lured away chasing a runaway sheep who has no desire to stay, the Shepherd ultimately abandons those whom he was entrusted to cover, care for and protect. His absence to chase a sheep which has no desire to neither return, nor be caught simply opens the door for roaming wolves to come in and divulge that which he has been assigned to protect.

Many times we make the mistake of missing the context of correctly correlating the text in the Bible where it says, "allow the wheat and the tares to grow together", in thinking that we are to wait until the harvest for the separation to begin activation. The critical and crucial key is to separate wheat and weed the moment you identify the weed. If it's not cut off at the initial point of discovery, there will be no harvest as the weed will choke the life out of what would have "been" wheat.

Now, this is not a part of the book, but as I would say to young Preachers and Pastors, this is extra. Try to make sure you always communicate a text in context, as a text out of context is a pre-text and that's one of the primary principles of preaching which you never even want to penetrate. When any text is taken out of context and not presented in its proper presentation, you get conned and that cripples, and never communicates the crystal clear clarity which needs to be conceived.

This raises another pertinent and powerful point on which to present a platform. Understand in ministry, that a revolving door is not uncommon for unsettled sheep. One thing you will grow to know in your Ministry infancy, and in some cases, even the seasoned seasons, your Ministry may seem like a revolving door without roots of retention, but know that the revolving door results and responses have nothing to do with your Ministry readiness. It is the reality of "right time" versus "ripe time" as it pertains to the people present on the premises.

It may be your season of Harvest and "right time", but if your right time is not the followers "ripe time", it may cause conflict as opposed to cohesion. Bottom line, never take "personal" what ain't "purpose" in the first place. As the WORD communicates with crystal clear clarity, "lay aside every weight which so easily besets you" and this means departure that drives toward destiny.

Chapter Five

THE MOMENTARY MINISTRY "HOLY HONEYMOON"

U nderstand the make-up of Ministry from the micro-scope of TOTAL inclusion and all inclusive full picture view. There will be one segment which I will place a highlight and bright light on, which I refer to as the "Holy Honeymoon" moment and season. Giving a testimony inclusive of experience, there will be a shifting and a stormy season producing the opposite of Heaven, a Hell filled with hail, hits, hurts and hurdles. The perfect biblical and scriptural example is the Triumphant Entry of Jesus on what we refer to as Palm Sunday, when Jesus rode into town to the setting of a celebration, parade, branches being waved and thrown down in the streets to create a path and entrance of royalty afforded to a King. This was how His week started, one of the highest moments most would ever experience.

It was epic, but it also took only a few days for the tide to shift when the people discovered that His Mission was not theirs. Jesus never came to flip the script of the political structure of Roman rule and occupation, but He was simply finishing the assignment for which He came to fulfill per the will of His father and even prophetic preannouncement per Old Testament prophecy. In Ministry, you'll be amazed how quick the folks who began with you, expeditiously begin to abandon you when they feel the chips are not falling in their favor.

So, if you're a young Pastor or leader, understand the Seasons of your calling. Just like we discovered in the life of Joseph, palace may be the ultimate destiny of your journey, but there are "pit stops" before you park on the premises of promise and prosperity.

Providential path and assignment for Joseph was always destined to end with Palace authority, but there were preludes and pre-requisites required in the providential path which God had paved and poured. Joseph's journey began nothing like it would end.

Just remember, what GOD says will be, will be. You may have to experience a painful pit experience, a plot inclusive of a Potiphar's wife indecent proposal leading to false rape accusation, a (temporary) Prison Placement with the person in the prison being the petition to your parole. If you stay faithful and God Focused in YOUR response to the adversity, you WILL rise to your positional place, which was already providentially in place before you proceeded. Remember, Joseph learned to be content in whatever circumstance and situational state he found himself. Also, he never became ungodly, nor operated in retaliation. He continued to faithfully serve, even though he suffered throughout.

We can never step outside the WORD of God. We must allow God to do what He does as we continue to represent HIM. Keep the WORD close at all times and just as God promised to make our enemies (includes friendemies) our footstools, or in 2014 modern vernacular and colloquial communication, "make your hators your elevator," let GOD handle the discipline as you continue to drive with divine direction. Even more so, don't be shocked when the identity of those who try to dispose of you and deny your destiny is exposed. Many times those who seek to be closest, as opposed to those who have been divinely planted closest to you, often turn out to be the biggest obstacles for you.

You may try to walk a Jesus line most of the time, but in the final stretch and prior to your purpose being in permanent park, the possibility and rude reality is that you will discover a Judas at your table who has transacted a deal to sell you out, and a Peter who has never solidly bought into who you are. Just know that there may very well be a night time garden moment, and a down moment. You cannot afford to forget the omniscience of GOD in knowing ALL, which thereby only qualifies HIM to make your destiny call.

If God said it, it will not return void. The enemy knows that he is on a leash and whatever happens to you, God either allows it or authorizes it. The WORD communicates with crystal clear clarity that GOD will not test us beyond that which we are able to handle.

As a child of GOD, that simply and scripturally says to me, "If I'm IN it, I can WIN it." The bottom line is the enemy knows he can't deny your destiny. His best shot is to try to have you succumb to your situation, throw in the towel, and take the advice of a friend with the characteristics of Job's wife, curse God and die. In other words, the enemy knows he can't delete, deny nor take it, so he does all he can to entice and encourage you to give it up.

Just remember, what the enemy meant for bad, God worked it out for your good. It's truly a Faith walk and our strength comes from solid supporting scripture. Praise God for the Apostle Paul and his words per Romans 8:28, "and we know that all things work together for good for those who are called according to His purpose." First this is afforded to an exclusive audience and not available to anybody. It is folks of faith, those called according to HIS purpose.

Now as I park on the premises of this passage and peek at the pertinent particulars, the intro of this text reveals a powerful and potent Faith statement, "and we know". This powerful proclamation points out that this is not something we need to doubt, despite the full fruition arrival with visible and visual display. So as folks of Faith, this scriptural statement shows us how the righteous rolls in faith and with faith. Here it is, "and we KNOW, therefore we see...NOT we see, therefore we know." Remember, we walk by Faith (the substance of things hoped for and the evidence of things not seen) and **NOT** by sight (having to see it to believe it.)

There will be a down moment in Ministry prior to our elevation into destiny. Just live by the words of Pastor Donnie McClurkin, "After you've done all you can, YOU just stand." The key is what Pastor John P. Kee shared with me during my one on one interview with him per my inquiry of how he reached the highest musical success. Pastor Kee said, "It was Faith and follow-through."

That is where the growth of blessing and the shifting from seed into fruit takes place. The blessing is that if you're faithful and focused, you will rise with more power than you had when you went down.

Allow me to Preach here for a second or two on the highest power, omnipotence. Praise God for our **New Testament** Jesus example of HIS coming UP with More Power than He went down with. It was very interesting. In the Old Testament, all power was always an ocular demonstration of an all-encompassing strength and might. One awesome example was Moses conquering Pharaoh, and the Lord showed He had all power when He clogged water flow and backed up the water on all sides, as He allowed the children of Israel to march through.

However, when Pharaoh and his hard taskmasters started their pedestrian march across the same geographical location, God allowed the waters back in and Pharaoh and his army drowned in the red sea. That was classic Old Testament omnipotence.

However, in New Testament omnipotence, it's just the opposite. It shows what has often been referred to as the weakness of GOD being stronger than the strength of MAN. Just remember Jesus, as God Man, going to Calvary and being hung high, stretched wide, nailed hands, nailed feet, pierced side and even died, but after death's best shot, HE still won with a Sunday Morning Victory. It's almost analogous to my getting in the ring with Floyd Mayweather and he says, "Pastor, go ahead and tie my hands, tie my feet, tie my back, now throw your best punch and Floyd simply nudges me with his shoulder and he still wins."

Remember you are on assignment and greater is the God that is within you than any force or opposition outside of you. Just stay faithful, focused and GOD's favor will forever follow. Matter of fact, this ecclesiastical escort entourage has names, "surely Goodness and Mercy shall follow you all the days of your life IF you dwell in the House of the Lord, forever."

Chapter Six

NIGHTMARE ON
WEST WASHINGTON STREET
"HE TOUCHED MY BABY"

This was the NIGHT of my biggest Ministry nightmare. The Church phone rang, my Executive Assistant had stepped away from her desk so I answered. It was a call from a young Lady whom I had watched grow up from a child. She was a young kid at the church where I served in my early 20's. She was now a beautiful, educated, independent young woman and a mother of two small children.

She was a former member of our church when I first began my Pastorate, active on our Administrative Team, YPD, Youth Quake staff and Music Ministry. She was still like family, as we had watched and even assisted in nurturing her babies and watching them grow from pampers into toddlers.

The whole moment seemed very dismal and dreary as I could sense in my spirit when the phone rang, that this was not going to be a normal call. She sounded as if she was fighting for breath and life. Her words were barely audible, as you could hear the piercing pain pouring from the words she was trying to push out. She said, "Pastor Brown, he touched my baby! Why would he do that? He touched my baby!!" I asked her who, and she screamed his name. My heart sank. This was a Pastor's nightmare. I immediately told her to call the police, get the baby to the hospital and I would meet her there. I arrived at the hospital just after she did. As with any mother, just getting off work and arriving to hear the numbing news involving the horrific and tragic occurrence with her baby girl, she was stunned, shocked and in a mental block and lock. Her baby girl was only 8 years old! I embraced her with a Pastor's love and offered my apology and consoling sympathy as best I could. There was not really much one could say, or what she would want to hear at that moment, other than "why." It was not a question anyone could answer, and surely the one who did it wouldn't answer.

I simply told her, I was there with her throughout whatever needed to be done to get her baby the treatment she needed and to ensure that this was reported immediately to EVERY appropriate authority.

As we were waiting anxiously to get her daughter examined, the medical staff came out and informed us the hospital did not have the rape kit equipment needed for situations of this nature and we were advised to go to

Cardinal Glennon Children's Hospital. Understanding the sense of urgency with this tragedy yet being still very fresh and not wanting to waste any time, the hospital staff told us that the Police department would also meet us there to handle the legal portion of this sad and sickening saga.

I personally drove the mother and daughter across the river to the hospital and remained with them until the examination was complete, police report taken and escorted them back to their home.

Understand the dual dynamics of this disgusting dilemma. This was not just a nightmare because of the sad, singular and sickening surface of which the inappropriate touching and violation of a child by a grown adult male took place. The fact that this person served in the role of Godfather for the years after her mother left our church; made it worst. This was a direct and personal hit to my Ministry which had always been insulated with integrity. This was a monumental mountain of misery by itself, but it was growing into a Pastoral nightmare for me personally because of the "he" whom the mother identified and called out when she initially alerted me of her horrific hit. The "he", was someone actively serving as the Youth Minister of our church.

After getting through that nightmare moment, the legal action was activated and the person was arrested. One thing you will grow to know in Ministry, it's never just about you as the Leader, but anyone connected to you in any concrete capacity places you at a risk by association until the dust settles and truth prevails. As I share all the time, your Integrity has to begin before your journey into destiny begins. One of the greatest things about integrity, is that it will stand for you even when your mental and emotional legs are too exhausted to elevate you into standing for yourself.

The nightmare on West Washington began, despite the fact that the horrific event never took place at the church. I did NOTHING but support the mother and child from the time of alert, although they had not attended in more than two years.

Pictures of my church, marquee and even our church van were splattered across news stations throughout the region and abroad on internet and social media sites. Nobody bothered to inquire about my immediate response upon notification, or support for the mother and child from notification to treatment. This tragedy truly devastated us all.

The next life changing phone call came the next day, as news was quickly spread across local, regional and even national news outlets. This was my second most unforgettable nighttime moment. I was working a hot project on my daytime job over 20 years at Scott AFB, and I received a call from someone whom I had grown up with, shared the same homeroom during our high school days at East St. Louis Senior High School "aka" East Side, and now she served in a major role for the local law enforcement agency. I was not just her classmate, but we grew up like family and truly lifetime friends.

She wanted to know if I could come to the Police Station to do an interview, as she had a reporter wanting to speak with me. She knew it was something I could pass on since I was not connected to any charges, but she also knew that it would probably be best for me to come. One mistake you never want to make with media is allowing them to speak for you on perception; and risk it not aligning with the truth and facts. I told her to give me an hour and I'd come.

It was the longest ride of my life. In what is normally a 30 min ride from Scott AFB to the East St. Louis, it seemed like a 30 year eternity. This heart sinking day is forever etched in my memory. It was during the Presidential campaign season and our current President was campaigning, and happened to be right across the river for a stop in St. Louis, Missouri.

When I arrived on the parking lot and saw all of the news media trucks, some with satellites atop, major radio station vans, print media persons, etc., I immediately thought all of this media fanfare was probably because of the Presidential campaign. I honestly thought, at the time, Senator Barack Obama, the Democratic Presidential candidate, had come across the river to meet with our Mayor, the Honorable Alvin L. Parks, Jr. Little did I know, all of this media mob was just for me!

As I entered the building, deeply distraught over this whole dilemma, I could only pray as I tried to get up this flight of stairs with all of these aggressive, feisty reporters trying to grab an exclusive, as I was simply trying to get this over and done with. As I turned the corner of the public stairwell in the City Hall rotunda, I couldn't proceed without addressing this shocking statement from one of the arresting officers. Having been an advocate for youth since I was a youth and a positive role model in the community, it was time to establish my purpose for being present. I know the Police officer meant well but I was appalled when he tried to explain to me "This was not a witch hunt or unmerited attack against my Youth Minister, but this guy was dirty and the DNA had confirmed it." I was speechless and simply said, "do you think I would come to defend these disgusting and despicable acts against a baby? I'm about, protecting against this type of craziness."

Then came the most difficult interview of my life. I knew the layout of City Hall very well since I often taped my Teen Talk Television Show in the City Council Chambers and Conference Room. I knew you entered from the rear and walked to the front where the podium was located. I figured I had time to pray one last time, gather my thoughts and catch my breath before addressing what seemed like a media lynch mob at the time. Was I ever in for a shocker.

When I entered the room, television cameras and reporters were aimed at the door to follow my every move and breath upon my entrance The podium already had live radio and television mikes affixed to capture each and every word. My heart sunk as I was stunned by this setting and yet still grieving over the terrible tampering, touching and emotional damage done to a baby, whom I felt was truly one of my own. As I stood there, with my youngest sister standing behind me with tear filled eyes and praying through her own personal pain, as she had babysat and been like a mother to the child when the mother and kids attended our church.

The LORD showed up and took over the script previously planned. Nobody in the room understood at the time how things shifted, but I was praying for the opportunity to have the media hear my heart and feel the pure pulse of my person. GOD heard my plea and honored that on the spot.

In the twinkling of an eye, it happened and someone said, "Pastor, we know there are a lot of questions for you, so why don't we allow you to speak first." I knew this was truly supernatural intervention and spiritual interception, as the media wanted to throw in suspicion and implication as it related to my character and credibility. I immediately shared how I felt about what had tragically transpired. I shared without restraint nor restricted edits, that I felt these actions by a grown adult male and trusted Godfather guardian were despicable and disgusting and that this Minister was immediately demoted to a former Minister under my leadership and church. I shared that although I was not present, nor had any connection to this horrific incident, it was still very personal. I felt I had let one of my baby's down by not having suspected and detected this as even a possibility with the person.

One of the questions asked by a reporter also gave me an opportunity and public platform on which to give a quick course on Church 101. She asked, "How could I have someone sitting in such close proximity, my pulpit, and not detect nor suspect the possibility of this behavior?" I shared with her and the huge media gathering, "Church folks never come with full exposure and transparency. They arrive in disguise of who they truly and completely are. Many hope they get delivered before they get discovered. People don't arrive with true identity nametags like pervert, rapist, child molester or drunkard affixed. They come dressed in churchy attire like WWJD t-shirts, fancy bible covers, large crosses and disguises." I went on to say that as a Pastor, I was in the field of giving second chances and encouraging others to maximize their potential and positive possibilities.

The one point which truly hit home and silenced the room was when I spoke of entities that specialize in background checks, scrutinizing history and personal past. That entity is law enforcement agencies.

The atmosphere shifting twist in this case was that the agency that actually arrested the perpetrator, was the same agency which issued him a city weapon, and a badge. He was actively serving in the capacity of Auxiliary Police Officer for the city despite investigation and arrest.

From that point on, the inquiry shifted from a media circus looking to attack me personally as another example of a Church Scandal and a Pastor sidestepping; to declining comment and/or sending a scripted spokesman. It shifted due to the shock and surprise of encountering someone who came communicating in concrete, complete candor, and integrity, as an advocate. The exact opposite of the normal dodging, ducking, bobbing and weaving, standard responses usually given by Pastors in the past. In the post formal interviews, many of the media members said to me, they were shocked that I even attended, when I could have declined since I was not connected, other than having had the person serve on my staff.

They didn't know it was not an option, because this was not about a single isolated incident, but EVERY Church and Pastor who stands was on trial. Once again, to either answer the mail of this issue or continue to sweep it under the rug and give an appearance of perpetrator protectors. I knew I was the voice and face of young people for a generation in the entire region and answering the bell and the mail was a must.

This event was my most difficult hour. It was not only the hour in which I grew the most spiritually in Faith and strength, but also in getting a revelation of what constitutes true friends. I can identify with Jesus when He saw firsthand when the trial and trouble really came, those closest to Him sought to flee and flight.

It was truly a dark season for me personally and corporately, as many supporters including Pastors shared they had no doubt about me having any involvement in the incident, but just as a caution, thought and said "Let's postpone our scheduled calendar events until this passes over and the smoke clears."

I understood one national grant provider, as the eyes of present and prospective donors, wanted to ensure their donations for Teen Talk Television were not going to an organization of someone who had connections with the very tragedy and indiscretions he spoke against. The funding considerations were suspended until it was crystal clear there was no connection whatsoever! Praise GOD they hung around for the facts and our reunion was highlighted with several thousand dollars of funding being awarded.

The personal connections were the ones which brought the deepest disappointment. These persons had years of the proof and passion I possessed for people; especially children and youth. I was devastated as anybody that truly knew me, knew I was always an advocate and solid supporter for youth.

This season was not only tough for me from the masses and media; but it was one of the toughest moments because of the reaction from some of my members. Many understood the endless Love for one who was so near and dear to us while serving in our Ministry. Unfortunately, they did not appear to understand the law and legal liability at even implying anything other than disgust for the despicable acts and indecencies which had taken place. Due to the serious nature of the crime, a Class X Felony, it was critical that the church be unified in denouncing this crime and maintain a firm position on actually where we stood on the issue. Looking from just the surface of the situation and without having the cold hard facts of the details and depth of the aggravated sexual abuse of this 8 year old baby, with DNA confirmation, there appeared to be reasonable doubt. This doubt was based on what we had actually witnessed in visible behavior from the minister prior to this act.

The point I was trying to impress upon my members was I had all the facts, which were not even privy to public release, as the investigation was ongoing. It was believed there were at least two more victims. This separated me from the surface surveyor's as my stand was based on pure facts. It was never an issue of me throwing him under the bus or abandoning him on a mere accusation. The test of proof (DNA) had been taken and the results confirmed that the accusation was accurate. From a legal aspect for our church, these waters could have potentially opened up a floodgate of liabilities for lawsuits and litigation if they were not treaded upon with caution and compliance with counsel.

Knowing all those critical factors, it did not behoove us to visit, write, attempt to communicate nor anything of that nature, unless it took place after the legal conviction or acquittal. Also, any actions or implied support would not only hurt the victim who would be scarred for the rest of her life even further. It would have also crippled the credibility of our congregation collectively and me personally as one who had always been a child advocate. In addition to that, there were legal counsel advisements which had to be followed without deviation or the church would create severe legal risks.

It was very tough trying to communicate the seriousness of that aspect in the present when many were still locked into the relationship they knew to be in the past. During that dark, dismal hour of my life, I was asked daily if I heard how he was doing, but there were minimal to zero inquiries about how I was doing. I often wondered if the concern for him would have been the same if it had been their child that he touched.

Suffering daily through the toughest emotional moment of my life, it was a huge pill to swallow, but God kept me through the storm until all doubts were lifted and the truth came out in the conviction with a 30 year prison sentence. There were no winners in this dark chapter and it was time for healing for everyone.

It was never a situation of the Love being instantly disconnected. It was simply dealing with the crisis which was created by the crime, the consequences which came as a result of corrupt choice, and full compliance with the correct legal communications that did not open up our church for major legal liabilities.

Once everything was done, all the facts were compiled, conviction and sentencing was imminent, the phone calls returned and I respectfully declined any present or future affiliations with those who excused themselves from friendship during the difficult, trying and turbulent times. One thing you will grow to know, the people who truly love you will be there with you and for you. True friends and supporters stand with you throughout the storm.

One of my greatest Ministerial Mentors, the Rev. Dr. Claude E. Shelby, Sr., and one who continues to bless me with the golden opportunity of facilitating the major Midwest Youth Quake revival, which began early in my ministry and has since grown to several thousand, for the past 10 years showed it better than anyone. Pastor Shelby another spiritual father and supporter was briefed in depth and detail about the disgusting dilemma.

Never once did he raise or even slightly suggest doubt because he had witnessed my integrity from a very young age, as a Preacher and person. He also knew the root from which came the fruits, as he grew up in the same small town of Brooklyn (Lovejoy), Illinois with my Grandmother who raised me, long before I was even thought of. He didn't have to say it. He showed it by welcoming me just a month after, as if none of this nightmare had ever taken place. There was never even a discussion, as Papa Shelby knew the young man he had watched and assisted in mentoring and molding. For others, who chose to stand on the safe side until they felt sure, it was evident more than ever the time to terminate those relationships had come. Those persons had failed the test of friendship miserably and this was a learning lesson and discovery moment.

Just a point to note, "If someone will abandon you at your lowest moment, they definitely don't deserve to share and celebrate with you in your future highlight moments."

Chapter Seven

EXPECT DELIVERANCE
BUT ALSO EXPECT DELILAH

As we travel behind the church doors and examine the entire picture with depth and detail, you will discover the duality reality revealed in the spiritual and carnal components. Understand this powerful and pertinent principle, if you're preaching an unadulterated Word to the people, there will be spiritual and supernatural harvest coming forth, by faith, in the form of deliverance. When you plant the seed of truth, it makes us free as the bible communicates with crystal clear clarity, "ye shall know the truth and the truth shall make us free."

Just as you come to expect the deliverance in spiritual harvest, you can also expect Delilah to come in carnal craziness. The enemy never ceases to crack your credibility and create doubt about your authenticity, legitimacy and integrity. Unfortunately, there are still some Delilahs looking to deceive while consistently and continually coming from an angle of dangle. You'll be amazed at the boldness exhibited when Delilah dives in determined to take you down.

Never underestimate the extent or extreme that assassins will go to; in trying to amputate your anointing and discredit what divine deposit has credited. In just ten years, I have experienced some attempts so bold, it left me dizzy and wondering, "Did that really just happen?" Never forget that every meeting has a mission and many times the mission is anything but ministry. Often it's an attempt to create a situation of manipulation, ultimately leading to expiration in your credibility and character. Be very careful because some will use what has your heart the most as a smokescreen to get at what they deeply desire the most. That's you and NOT the God in you and of you.

This true story from my personal Pastoral journal will help place some meat on the bone of the point I just made.

Anybody that knows me already knows when it comes to preaching and children, I'm as soft as a sponge as those are my true loves. On one occasion, there was a child who showed strong signs of possibly having a calling to preach on his life, just as I had around the same time, when I was his age. I was never blessed as some of my peers were to have a Father as a Pastor growing up, and to be a 3rd or 4th generation Preacher. I came as a solo.

The idea of possibly having an adopted spiritual son and training him up as I would have given anything to have when I was coming into my calling, was truly a dream come true. I proceeded to have weekly classes with the young man and just started out sharing biblical lessons, praying and seeking God for confirmation of a calling on his life to preach the Gospel or simply a kid with a zeal for Word instruction. This potentially promising young man was the son of a single parent and all of our weekly sessions were held in my office.

One day the young man came in and said, "My mother said that you don't have to keep having these sessions here at the church because you're always here, and you can come to our house and do them. She said that it also gives you a break and you can come down to our house, relax and she can even fix dinner." I shared with the young man, that should he become a Preacher and eventually a Pastor that was a huge no-no in going to a single woman's home.

As far as the immediate invitation from his mom, I told him that would not be appropriate. I said, "Please let your mom know that I have to decline her offer and that our present place would continue to be the best place."

I thought that would squash all of that discussion, but the following Sunday his mother came and asked me, "Did my son tell you what I said about coming over?" I reiterated what I shared with her son. I never revisited the discussion and eventually the mother took her son and left the Church.

On another occasion, probably one of the boldest ever, a young lady was so bold that she requested a meeting, was not even a member, but simply came to discuss appearing as a guest on one of my television shows. She arrived with a deeply cut, tight fitted body shirt, revealing an elevated cleavage console with full display and literally armed with a personal presentation bag that included chocolate kisses, candles and other personal items.

My staff was stunned, speechless and in total shock. It was so bold that it was comedic but also pathetic, as we witnessed the evidence of the extreme extent exhausted in this effort. It was truly a very quick meeting as the underlying agenda was very visible and quite strong on the surface.

On another occasion, the person used more of a slow and subtle strategy. A middle-aged woman lady that visited for several Sundays without ever formally uniting, requested a meeting with me to share where she was as far as interest and future in the church. She spoke for nearly two hours about being from out of town, not really having a reason to remain in town but she was now, for the very first time in her life, being led to park, come off the pew and become a participating parishioner within our church.

She said she was ready to work but needed guidance as to the best fit and area of need. The meeting was growing quite lengthy with no new points arising and fatigue from my 18 hour day was setting in. As we approached the second hour, I was spiritually sensing and discerning that the discussion was not the deeply desired discussion which she really sought. I proceeded to end the session and my last question truly exposed her real reason for the meeting.

I asked her was there anything else other than what we had discussed the last two hours, and she stated there was. I asked her to elaborate and she went into a posture of "This is so embarrassing." My mood was now shifting, as I could clearly see where this was headed.

I simply shared there was no reason to get embarrassed now, and asked her to explain. She proceeded and went on to ask me, "Did I notice her when she first came to the church?" I was floored and wanted to make sure I was hearing what she was asking. I wanted to be absolutely sure that I was rightly receiving what I heard being transmitted in correct context and candor. After she confirmed that was the case, I simply shared with her that when I enter the sanctuary on Sunday morning, all I see are sheep and spiritual needs. I never enter the House of Worship seeking to be anything other than a Man of God and God's Pastor for His people. As much as I was floored, I had tremendous respect for the woman as she simply left the church. She never returned to seek a change of heart, convince me otherwise or to create a climate of conflict and craziness.

Behind the walls of the church will come all kinds of characters, and most come directly after the leader; the one they perceive to have the strength or whom they see as the Samson. The truth of the matter is, with an all-out attack on the church and the desire to cut off the head, you will probably see more Delilahs than you'll ever see in Deliverances.

Learn to guard the door and train your staff to "watch and pray" as they guard the camp. Most attempts are so bold, there is no time wasted in working in the fields. These persons come straight to the inner court presenting a posture to park as close to the Pastor as possible. Some will be obvious as they will share samples and bait to get a feel, while others will go undercover for months and even years. Never stop having a watchful eye as signs and hints will reveal sooner or later.

One of my uneventful memorable moments made a believer out of me. On one occasion, a new young lady came up to join our church and gave what seemed like a First Lady Acceptance speech.

She was not the least bit shy as she shared with the congregation that she had done her homework on me, knew how awesome I was, knew I would receive her but her only concern was how they, "our congregation" would receive her.

Being who I am, wanting to always believe the best comes out of everyone if you give them a chance; I gave her the benefit of the doubt. It was only a matter of time before the young lady found an unrelated reason to satisfy and justify a good excuse for leaving. She was able to save face and she moved on.

Whether it's having someone hug you in what appears to be a holy embrace while dropping her travelling hand behind you, underneath the communion table ledge you're leaned up against, to grope your behind and flip a wink; or another one sliding her house key in your pocket during a revival with times for access possibility attached or the all-time most bold move in my lifetime of a woman coming out of every ounce of clothing, refusing to dress or leave unless you give in and forcing you to audition for Joseph part 2 with a Forrest Gump encore, "run Forrest run" response. Temptation will come and you must practice in the pre-season to be faithful and stay clear of situations which seeks to force you into fumbles and futility.

These are just a few of the true stories, which could have very easily been tragic endings, had I not been grounded in GOD. A word to Pastors and leaders leaning toward this journey, "Make sure you're God grounded before you get going." My Grandmother raised me to never forget the value of reputation. She would often tell me, "It takes years to build up but you can lose it in seconds."

As a young, bachelor Pastor, I can testify first hand, you must implement intensive insulation from the ongoing dangling of Delilah type temptations. One of the greatest things about my office at the church is the huge window which opens to my adjacent Administrative Team's office. During counseling, they may not be able to hear the dialogue but they can see the positions of the persons present.

My seat is always at the huge desk or the large chair facing the window into the adjacent office. I'm visible at all times and there's never a doubt of where I am in the room.

It's not a matter "if" the temptation will come. Even after fasting and praying multiple days, it will come. If the enemy would tempt the Son of God, how vulnerable are we to be fresh for the picking? With each level comes another devil and elevation comes from the passing of Divine examination. The enemy will tempt but, GOD will test as a faith that cannot be tested is a faith which cannot be trusted for next level promotion. God has to see if we're live or Memorex. If we're focused and faithful, we'll pass with flying colors and favor will follow, as it is the fruit which comes from the faithfulness factor.

Once again, never forget that every meeting has a mission and not all missions have ministry mindsets, but many have manipulation motivated outsets. Embrace the deliverances but excommunicate the spirits of the Delilahs.

Chapter Eight

"THE GLUE IN STAYING TRUE ~ INTEGRITY"

The key to surviving the events and experiences which truly take place in the reality of the totality behind the church doors, inclusive of the good, bad and ugly, is staying faithful and focused as God's favor will flourish in your favor. The WORD of God reiterated this thematic thread by declaring, "If we're faithful over a few things, He'll make us ruler over many." Don't get caught off guard with a personal perception created solely from hopeful expectations of everything being all roses. There will be a ton of distractions which derive by demonic design, as the devil wants to destroy that which was meant to divinely employ. Stay faithful despite how things look. Life is a session of seasons and every portion and part has its place and purpose as it pertains to providential path. When it comes to members, many will come but also many may leave as many are called but few are chosen to be permanent fixtures in the final package.

I stand as an example of experience with resume proof. In only 10 years of ministry, 6 associate ministers, the first 3 ordained deacons, as well as the next 3 deacons who were in training and never made it to ordination, are no longer with us. Less than a dozen of the members who began with us, remain with us, in what is our most fruitful and present productive season. It's not that any of those preceding seasons should have never taken place, it simply means that the preceding persons were simply present for a season and when their respective seasons were complete, closure of those chapters was correct.

Of course some of those seasons did not end as pleasant and pleasing as a Pastor would pray they would. However, valuable lessons were learned, and it helped shape and strengthen me into a Leader whose learned firsthand how to turn lemons into lemonade.

As a young Leader, remember the best lemonade comes from actual lemons. When life or people give you lemons, make lemonade. Many of the frustrations from former members who refused to follow helped mold and make me into a master lemonade maker.

Remember that God ultimately gives His leader the vision and when He truly gives vision, it comes with provision. Many times you will discover behind the doors, ulterior motives, hidden agendas or those persons who think pertinent places and positions are available for purchase.

Be very weary of those who work extra hard to be close to you personally and not purposely. You will soon discover, once you do not step outside of Lead and follow their lead, they will look to leave. Take this departure as a blessing of relief from what would have grown to be a burden of weeds eventually choking out wheat.

One thing I can testify without any reservation whatsoever is that God will provide. I witnessed it firsthand from a front row seat in live experience. In an ironic twisting turning point, one of our biggest member turnovers came after one of our most successful building campaigns.

It was a strange season where GOD led me to make a call that had doubt dousing behind the doors and inside the inner walls. I had just returned from a major Pastor's Conference and the word or theme for 2012 was that we were in one of the toughest economic times in our nation's history and Pastors should refrain from any projects for renovations/extensions. Even more, we were told that it would behoove us to look immediately at executing every cost saving option. I returned in full agreement on the wisdom linked with these words given. Then, just as I returned home, God gave me "my" direct dispatch from

HIS desk, which said to renovate. Here I sat like Arnold, in a "Diff'rent Strokes" segment, "What you talking about GOD" daze. I responded as if GOD had missed the memo on our refraining from renovations.

I admit I forgot for a second and said, "God, we were just told to refrain from anything and God instantly spoke into my spirit... that was the WORD for the others, but your WORD is to go forward and show that you can reap in a recession, if I have ordained the season to be your season of Harvest." That was the first shocker.

So off we go with this leap of Faith. The vision initially began with simply a flat roof replacement for our Administrative Wing at a cost of 20k. Understand, we had no "K's" at that point. As God was giving me the seed formula to go forward, He began pointing out that the parking lot, which was an eyesore for years, needed to be paved and striped; with a Buckingham gate accented with gold finials. From that, I was shown a Parking Lot sign, full face lift of all interior hallways, carpeted hallways, wine and crème décor throughout the complex, crystal chandeliers, green side entrance corridor floors with gold flakes, cherry wine staircase accented with gold flakes going up to our 3rd level, gold plated edges on each set of steps, complete demolition of our exterior concrete porches, new custom handrails and sidewalks, updated Teen Center with professional SJ39 NFL autographed paraphernalia and professional plastered computer training center and upgrades to all 18 rooms and 7 bathrooms, including a new custom tiled floor for the lower level Banquet Center. The price for all of these renovations rose from $20,000 to $80,000.00. I was speechless but trusting God all the way as I knew vision came with provision.

The next detail which truly floored me and nearly sent my faith into complete cardiac arrest was when GOD informed me that the 80K also came with a 90 day limit. It was June of 2012 and we had what appeared to be an insurmountable task before us, with a due date by the

Divine of October, 90 days. Some say when God shows up, He always shows out. But this was a modern day miracle move taking place.

As several key persons began attempts to hold us hostage and demanding ransom of control by withholding their pledge, God continued to show up and show this was of HIM and not them. God led a concerted crusade of persons outside the doors to pour resources into the place to meet every invoice need. Nearly 75% of this 80k price tag was paid by folks outside the doors and persons who had watched me in Ministry since the day I started my Kids Church Ministry. It was a harvest from seeds of service which began long before this day.

My first boss Chief Harold "Ray" Collins, a retired 30 year CMSgt. and nearly 20 year Civil Servant retired, saw something in me at 20 and began with sowing the first 5k and sealing it with the final 15k. Once again, had I not shown integrity early, there would be no harvest or blessing later.

This was indeed a historic and monumental turning point in the life and legacy of our church, as dedication of all of the above took place on schedule, October 2012. It also marked turnover of several persons who decided their time of departure had come for reasons which add no value or worth in holding a discussion. As I said early, every person and everything had their season.

In the end, GOD prevailed, every need was met, mission was accomplished and faces may have changed but Favor never faltered. Our church began with a major deficit, but now shares deliverance and dynamic destiny, after a decade for the world to see. Truly God gets the Glory and we simply Praise HIM for being a part of the story.

The reason for this book being written at this time and in this season, was to share some of what really happens behinds the doors. Never fail to forget, if you're faithful, God will deliver you into HIS ordained destiny for your life, while bringing you through the total package which includes all three, the GOOD, the BAD and even the UGLY. You're on your way when you have the total picture presentation.

~THANK YOU~

C ompleting this author assignment, in this season, has truly been a huge humbling honor for me. First and foremost, to GOD be the Glory for guiding me through HIS flow for each and every chapter. Secondly, I Praise God for my personal editor, Lady Catherine V. Suggs, not only my Executive Administrative Assistant and Church Administrator but also my best friend and most LOYAL and FAITHFUL supporter from day one to present. Thank you for spending weeks and endless hours reading, editing and making sure my grammatical bases were covered. Last and surely not least, one who I refer to as "my brilliant little Brother", Levi "Too" King. This multi-gifted Brother is the creative mind behind one of the most eye catching book covers to ever land on a bookstore shelf. Not just with this book but website designs and one on one consultations. This was a monumental task coming out the gate but that load was lessened to the least weight possible because of this dynamic duo that aided and assisted my inaugural author season from pregnancy to birth. I'm eternally grateful and I'm already preparing on the next one.

Forever Grateful, Forever GOD:
Pastor Willie D. Brown

~IN MEMORY OF MY MATERNAL MENTORS~

Mother: Mrs. Camella "Mel-Baby" Brown

June 3, 1940 — May 17, 1991

Grandmother: Mrs. Claudia "Boopie" Watson-Jackson

CPSIA information can be obtained at www.ICGtesting.com
Printed in the USA
LVOW02*0725060814

397750LV00002B/14/P

9 781498 404242